Picasso

Maison de la Pensée Française,
2 Rue de L'Elysée

Exposition de Céramiques
du 8 mars au 30 juin
Picasso

POSTERS

PAIX
DÉSARMEMENT
POUR LE SUCCÈS
DE LA
CONFÉRENCE AU SOMMET
PARIS, MAI 1960
LE MOUVEMENT DE LA PAIX

Mourlot - PARIS

Picasso
POSTERS

Maria Costantino

PRC

This edition first published in 2001 by
PRC Publishing Limited,
The Chrysalis Building
Bramley Road, London W10 6SP

An imprint of **Chrysalis** Books Group plc

ISBN 1 85648 683 4

Printed and bound in China

Page 1: *Picasso Ceramics Exhibition
Poster,* 1958

Page 2: *Peace,* 1960

Contents and List of Plates

Introduction

Born in 1881 in Malaga in Spain, Pablo Picasso was one of the most original, creative and prolific artists of the twentieth century. Although best known for such paintings as *Guernica* and as the originator of Cubism, Picasso worked in a variety of other media including sculpture, ceramics, murals, theater design, as well as writing plays and poetry. While much has been written about Picasso's work in these other fields, Picasso's activity as a poster designer has largely been overlooked and ignored.

While the sheer volume of Picasso's paintings means that they tend to dominate exhibitions and monographs, we should not ignore the fact that he produced as many posters as his contemporaries Braque, Léger, Miró, Chagall and Matisse combined. But despite this fact and the recent studies and reappraisals of the works of the great poster artists like Jules Chéret, Toulouse-Lautrec, Paul Colin and Cassandre, to name but a few, Picasso's posters have yet to receive widespread recognition.

In 1900 Picasso, who had grown up in the avant-garde artistic climate of Barcelona, helped to found *Juventut*, an art journal which expressed the desire to

break down the barriers that existed between the various arts. Given this early aim it should come as no surprise that Picasso should venture into other media than painting. As the poster began to be recognized as an art form from the late nineteenth century, a growing number of fine artists were attracted to the medium.

As early as 1847 fine artists like Gavarni were producing posters. He was followed shortly afterwards by Eugène Delacroix and Honoré Daumier, who produced one of the first commercial posters following a commission from a coal-storage company. The poster as an independent art form was, however, really disregarded until the later part of the nineteenth century following the contributions to the field, particularly by Jules Chéret (1836-1932) and Henri de Toulouse-Lautrec (1864-1901).

Working at the Chaix Studios in Paris, Chéret was to become known as the father of the modern poster and a pioneer of color lithography. While the subject matter of Chéret's posters consisted invariably of pretty girls swathed in skirts and petticoats – subjects that were drawn from the long tradition in French painting and exemplified best by artists like Fragonard and Boucher – Chéret's use of color was bold and bright and was achieved by using four or five colored printing blocks. Recognition for both Chéret and the poster came in the form of France's highest honor, the award of the Légion d'Honneur, awarded to Chéret for creating a new 'branch' of art.

A contemporary of the Chaix Studio of artists, Toulouse-Lautrec was no doubt influenced by Chéret, but like Gauguin and Van Gogh, he was more impressed by the techniques of the Japanese printmakers whose works had been introduced into Europe in the 1860s and 1870s.

It was Pierre Bonnard (1876-1947) who introduced Lautrec to the art of poster making in 1891. A co-member of the Nabis group, Bonnard himself produced his first poster for the art journal *La Revue Blanche* in 1894. The journal contained illustrations of the works of Bonnard, Vuillard, Lautrec and Maurice Denis, and ran successfully for twelve years. In 1901 *La Revue Blanche* discovered and supported the young Picasso.

Lautrec's use of large flat areas of color emphasized the composition and construction of his posters while he took as his subject matter the entertainers of the

chair and with pictures on the walls. It has been suggested that this print is a sort of self-portrait set at the café El Quatre Gats with Picasso in the guise of a bullfighter. The theme of bullfighting in Picasso's work at this time is restricted solely to this small etching, but the theme was to reappear not only in his paintings but in the posters made in France after 1945. Although it was not until 1904, when Picasso moved to Paris, that he took up etching once more, the outcome of his earlier efforts was *The Frugal Repast* (etching, 1904, 18¼ × 14¾ inches). Belonging to the Blue Period, *The Frugal Repast* shares the theme of blindness and poverty earlier expressed in paintings like *The Blind Man's Meal* (1903).

It was during a visit to Paris in October and November of 1900 that Picasso became familiar with the works of modern French masters such as Lautrec and Degas whose subjects of the 'social milieu' of Parisian barmaids, prostitutes, dancers, outcasts, and beggars, Picasso was to transplant into his own works in the Blue Period (1901-04).

Following this trip Picasso returned to Spain, first to Madrid for a few months, and then to Barcelona, where, back in the society of friends at the El Quatre Gats, Picasso produced his first poster. This poster depicts a group of regular clients at the café seated and standing around one of the tables, while at their feet lies a dog. In the manner of Toulouse-Lautrec, Picasso has signed his name simply as a 'P' enclosed by a circle. In most respects this first poster though competent in its treatment of the figures and the overall composition, does not give any indication of the powerful creativity to come.

Picasso's next major achievement in graphic work came in the 1930s. In the Paris ateliers of Eugène Delâtre, Louis Fort and Roger Lacourière, Picasso was shown the various techniques of etching and aquatinting.

In etching, originally a method of decorating armor, a polished surface of a metal plate is covered with a thin layer of ground made up of molten waxes, gums and resins. By drawing through this ground with a metal point, the metal plate beneath is exposed. The plate is then im-

Parisian cabarets and the life of the 'demimonde.' In 1891 Lautrec designed his first poster for the cabaret, *Le Moulin Rouge*, the celebrated venue of the infamous dance 'Le Can-Can.' In the following years and over thirty posters later, Lautrec had introduced the cabaret stars La Goulue, Jane Avril, Valentin, May Milton, Yvette Guilbert and Aristide Bruant. Beginning each poster with a series of preliminary oil studies, Lautrec often restricted himself to a simple silhouette drawn with as few lines as possible. Only when satisfied with the studies would he take the painting to the lithographers for printing. Lautrec's economy of line and elimination of all unnecessary details were to have a great influence on the poster designers who followed and were also to shape considerably the early work of Picasso.

During the 1930s the poster's importance was to be fully recognized. Poster competitions were set up by all the large organizations including the Salon d'Automne which created a new commercial art section. The works of the new

generation of poster artists including Charles Loupot, Jean Carlu, Paul Colin, Pierre Fix-Masseau and the great Adolphe Mouron (Cassandre), had finally achieved the deserved status in the arts.

Picasso's first venture into graphic art appears to have been initiated through his contact with a group of young artists and writers in Barcelona who congregated at a café-cabaret called El Quatre Gats (The Four Cats). In 1899 Picasso's friend Ricardo Canales suggested that he try making an etching on copperplate. The only print made during Picasso's 'Spanish Period' resembles a small painting as it was tinted with watercolors and then varnished. At this stage in his career, Picasso was signing his name 'Picasso Ruiz Picasso,' using both his father's (Ruiz) and mother's (Picasso) names; but from around 1900-1901 he was to drop his father's name completely. The print is inscribed El Zurdo (The Left-Handed Man) and the image is of a picador holding a lance, while at his feet sits an owl. Surprisingly, the bullfighter is not shown in the arena but inside a room furnished with a

mersed in a bath of acid which bites into the metal through the exposed lines. The depth of the line and its darkness when printed is determined by the length of time the plate is immersed in the acid. Since the soft ground covering the plate offers very little resistance, the artist has much the same freedom as in drawing. But etching does have some restrictions. The exposed areas cannot be more than the thickness of a line and the lines cannot be drawn too closely together because the acid will bite under the protecting ground between them causing the ground to collapse and the acid to flow and bite into the plate indiscriminately.

While etching is a method of producing lines, aquatint is essentially a tone process which can be used to imitate the appearance of watercolor works. The aquatint process was first devised by the Frenchman Jean-Baptiste Le Prince around 1768 and relies on the partial protection of the surface of a metal plate by a porous ground of powdered resin attached to the

Left: Toulouse Lautrec's poster for the novel *Reine de Joie* by Victor Joze.

Below: Paul Colin's poster for Vichy mineral water.

Below right: Cassandre's poster for the North Star train, 1927.

plate by heat. When etched the acid bites tiny rings around each grain of resin which hold enough ink when printed to give the effect of a wash. By 'stopping out' areas of the ground with varnish, pure white areas can be achieved. Graduations of tone can be made by carefully repeating the biting and varnishing processes. The disadvantage of aquatint is that it produces a 'negative' print, as the stopped-out areas remain white.

For a 'positive' print, an alternative process is sugar- or lift-ground aquatint. Here the plate is covered with resin but rather than cutting through it, the artist draws on the surface using a solution of sugar and water. After the whole plate is varnished, the plate is immersed in water which causes the sugar under the varnish to swell, lifting the area to be exposed. The plate is then bitten with acid and printed.

In 1936, using a combination of etching and aquatint techniques, Picasso produced some of his finest graphic works as illustrations for books such as Balzac's *Chef d'Oeuvre Inconnu*, Ovid's *Metamorphoses* and, in 1937, for Buffon's *Histoire Naturelle*.

In 1968 Picasso once again took up lift-ground aquatint for the illustrations to *La Célestine* by Fernando de Rojas. One of the first attributed stories in Spanish literature, *La Célestine* tells the tragi-

comic story of a doomed love affair between Melibea and Calixto. These 36 tiny illustrations were among the 347 intaglio prints Picasso completed during a seven-month burst of creative energy in 1968.

While intaglio printing was on the whole reserved for his prints, for his posters Picasso used two other print-making techniques: lithography and linocut.

Lithography, a process less than 200 years old, was invented in Munich in 1798 by Alois Senefelder and works on the principle that grease and water repel each other. Using a greasy medium, the artist draws on a granular surface, originally limestone from the Solenhofen region of Bavaria, now more frequently a specially grained alloy plate like zinc.

Once the greasy drawing is completed the surface is chemically treated to prevent the grease spreading and the stone or plate is dampened with water. This makes the surface reject the greasy printing ink except in the drawn areas where the ink is carried to the paper.

Although this process sounds rather hit and miss, lithographs can present a wide variety of appearances because as long as the drawing instrument is greasy, the slightest gestural nuances and ranges of tones are possible. Nineteenth- and twentieth-century artists such as Goya, Delacroix, Odilon Redon, Lautrec and Max

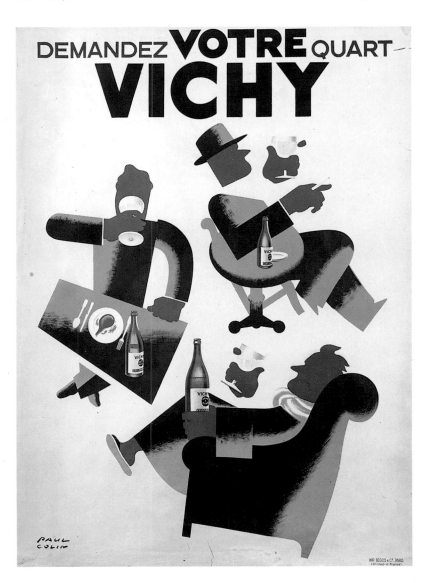

Ernst were to use a variety of tricks to create effects in their lithographs. Soft crayons were rubbed with chamois or the greasy image scratched with razor blades, pins and sandpaper. Lautrec created tones by spattering liquid grease from a toothbrush and Ernst took impressions from 'found objects' much as one would make a brass rubbing and transferred them to the printing surface.

In fact the stones or plates are so grease-sensitive that Picasso was able to 'draw' his children entirely from the grease-marks left by his fingerprints.

Commercial lithography developed throughout the nineteenth century and by the 1880s three-color half-tone photo-lithography had been achieved, followed in 1900 by offset lithography. Now litho-

graphs could be produced on a machine rather than by hand. The image is transferred from a curved metal plate on to a rubber blanket which in turn transfers the image on to paper. The rotary principle not only speeded up the number of prints produced but it also made it possible for the drawn image to appear on paper the right way round rather than in reverse as had been the case with the drawings on stones. Offset lithography was essentially the method that Picasso used when he made his posters, but occasionally he did return to traditional lithography, drawn on flat stones, as in the 1956 poster for the Galerie 65 in Cannes. The soft qualities that the stone surface can produce are here evident, especially in the lettering which is an integral part of all of

Above: Picasso's etching *The Frugal Repast* (1904) shares the theme of poverty with the earlier painting (above right), *The Blind Man's Meal* (1903).

Picasso's posters. Once again, the image of an owl reappears and here, with its rounded form, it is in keeping with the overall soft effects of the poster.

Before World War II Picasso occasionally turned his hand to lithography. In 1939 he produced a poster for the exhibition of costumes from Serge Diaghilev's Ballets Russes at the Musée des Arts Décoratifs in Paris which depicts a figure in a costume 'à la Chinoise' of red and violet tones. In 1916 Picasso had met the French poet, artist and film-maker Jean Cocteau who introduced him to the world of the Ballets Russes. The following year Cocteau persuaded Picasso to go with him to Rome and design the scenery and costumes for the ballet *Parade*. Choreographed by Léonide Massine with

music by Erik Satie and designs partly inspired by Cubism mixed with themes of Harlequins and the circus, *Parade* was termed by Guillaume Apollinaire a mixture of realism and 'Fantasy Surrealism'.

Picasso's links with the Ballets Russes were further strengthened in 1918 when he married one of Diaghilev's dancers, Olga Koklova. More ballet designs were to follow the next year for *The Three-Cornered Hat* with music by Manuel de Falla. The Spanish theme of the ballet provided Picasso with the inspiration for the drop curtain design based on the bullring.

It was in 1945 that Picasso's greatest lithographs were produced many of which were scenes of bullfights and still-life subjects. According to his life-long

friend and biographer, Jaime Sabartes, Picasso was attracted to the Paris print-making studio of Fernand Mourlot during the war primarily because Mourlot had a supply of firewood and could keep the studio comfortably warm. But once at the studios, Picasso discovered the artistic possibilities of lithography.

Mourlot's studio was housed in a large wood-frame building in the rue Chabrol near the Gare de l'Est. This building originally housed the printing firm of Honoré Bataille, founded in 1852. In 1940 Mourlot bought the Bataille plant and for a considerable period beginning in 1946 Picasso could be found working in the studios from eight in the morning until seven in the evening on a large number of lithographs; some were produced entirely

Left: *Café-Concert at the Ambassadeurs,* c. 1875-77 by Edgar Degas. Here Degas worked in pastel over a monotype. With a monotype, the image is painted on to a metal or glass base and transferred to paper, producing one unrepeatable print.

Right: One of Picasso's suite of 347 single etchings produced between March and October 1968.

Below right: Honoré Daumier's (1808-79) lithographic caricatures and satires commented on French society and morals. Here Daumier presents a view of a sleeping orchestra while above them on the stage the drama of a Greek tragedy continues unabated.

by his own hand and others with the assistance of one of Mourlot's highly skilled draftsmen. Picasso was not the only fine artist to work in the studios. Following the death of Fernand Mourlot, the printing firm passed to his sons and continued to attract artists of the caliber of Henry Moore and John Piper.

Following the liberation of Paris and the end of World War II, Picasso made his way from Paris back to the Mediterranean. On his arrival in the south of France he was offered the vast space of the Palais Grimaldi in Antibes as a studio. Although he continued to produce lithographic posters like the one from 1948 which was designed to advertise a series of lithographs that he had created as illustrations for Pierre Reverdy's book *The Song of the Dead* where in stark, simple terms Picasso conjured up the image of a small dog, Picasso met with difficulties of a practical nature in arranging for the transfer of stones and plates and proofs between Mourlot's studio in Paris and his home in the Midi.

The delays Picasso experienced made him impatient and eventually led him to make contact with Arnéra, a printer in nearby Vallauris, who was to linocut posters for him.

Linoleum is a floor covering made of a thick coating of oxidized linseed oil on a coarse cloth backing. After potato-cut printing, most school children have their first printing experience using linocuts, which is a very inexpensive technique. On the whole linocuts were disregarded by all but a handful of artists (such as Claude Flight and his circle in Britain in the 1920s), but Picasso used broad and strong marks made with a gouge, while in others he achieved subtle tones by lightly grazing the surface of the lino.

With the return to the Mediterranean, Picasso's subject matter changed abruptly. The still lifes of the war years which were permeated with a sense of foreboding and emblems of death such as shrouded figures and withered plants, gave way to more idyllic images of nymphs, fauns, centaurs, and satyrs who

dance and sport in Arcadian settings. Throughout all Picasso's works a new face appeared, that of Françoise Gilot, whose image Picasso frequently interpreted as a flower or the sun. In addition to being a model for his paintings and sculptures, Françoise, together with Picasso's children Claude (born 1947) and Paloma (born 1949) also appears in a 1953 poster (page 33) that is somewhat atypical of his poster works. The silhouettes of the models are here placed against a background of green, red and yellow bands of color which creates an abstract sky.

It was not until Picasso had established his home at the Villa la Galloise, an empty house adjacent to the village of Vallauris that he began to design posters in any substantial numbers. Picasso first went to Vallauris in 1936 driving around the region in the company of Yugoslavian photographer Dora Maar. In 1947 Picasso returned to the region, this time with his new love, Françoise Gilot, and settled at the villa until 1954 when Françoise walked out saying she did not want to spend the rest of her life with a historical monument.

Situated about 8 kilometers north-east of Cannes, Vallauris derived its name from the Roman settlement of Villa Aurea, which has been a center for flower, perfume and, most importantly, ceramics since Roman times. As early as the reign of the Emperor Tiberius, bricks were being fired in Vallauris. The pottery industry had been in decline in the region

since the turn of the century but was substantially revived after World War II by none other than Pablo Picasso.

Once settled in the area, it was not long before Picasso became interested in ceramics and was shown the various glazing and firing techniques by Suzanne Ramié who ran the Atelier Madoura. Many of the pieces that Picasso made were traditional forms – plates, dishes, pitchers and vases – but eventually his pottery was transformed into sculpture with works like Tanagras, so-called because they resembled classical statuettes, small figures which began their lives as bottles or vases, large heads and numerous 'Hellenistic' figurines of fauns, nymphs, satyrs and flautists.

With his contact at the Arnéra print works and his interest in ceramics, it comes as no surprise that Picasso's first posters were made in connexion with the potteries at Vallauris and many of the posters were advertisements for exhibitions at the village. Picasso's ceramic pieces were made in the shape of animals or decorated with their forms by incising and engraving the surface of the clay to reveal the underlying body color. Consequently Picasso's posters for the ceramics show reveal the discoveries he had made in areas like slip treatment of pottery. At times also the animals which decorated the pots also reappear on the posters.

The first poster commission for Vallauris in 1948 was part of the community's postwar effort to draw attention to the

Above: Picasso's study for the curtain for the *Three-Cornered Hat* (1919) designed for Serge Diaghilev's Ballets Russes.

Left: Picasso in his Paris studio.

Above right: *The Charnel House* (1944-45)

town, both as a resort center and as a production center for perfume and pottery, and many subsequent posters for Vallauris done by Picasso are variations on the same theme.

One of Picasso's favorite ceramic decorations was the motif of a satyr. Using a gouging tool on lino the faces of the satyrs are composed of three different forms and each eye is treated in a manner that their differences are compensated for by the variations in their shape.

For the most part, the posters advertising the ceramic exhibitions, like the

ceramics themselves, are executed in two colors.

In his first poster for Vallauris, the treatment is relatively traditional and, surprisingly for Picasso, symmetrical. Yet on closer inspection it is possible to see how the symmetry has in fact been broken by the addition of the black oval shapes over the eyes, nose and mouth of the satyr which create a further variety of shapes and forms, while on the lower right-hand side, one of the black lines had been completely omitted. In his approach to the same subject matter in two other posters, Picasso departed from the flat areas of color by introducing the further element of textural quality that looks rather like a wood-grain effect. Splitting the composition into two colors also helps to create the illusion of there being two planes on the same surface.

While the overlapping or interpenetrating planes are characteristic of Cubism, none of Picasso's posters is rendered in a completely Cubist technique. Throughout Picasso's life and works, once he had thoroughly investigated all the possibilities, theories and ideas available, he ended his explorations. Nevertheless,

Picasso never disregarded anything he had learnt and consequently, though he never returned to his earlier Cubism, certain ideas and touches were to reappear from time to time.

In the Vallauris exhibition poster of 1954 the technique of overlapping planes is once again apparent. At the same time the green and black tones are both foreground and background, as the shape of one vase is contained within the shape of a second, creating an illusion of depth without resorting to the use of traditional perspective.

In addition to posters advertising exhibitions of ceramics at Vallauris, Picasso also returned to a subject close to his heart, the bullfight. The increased popularity of the sport in France and its inevitable associations with Spain revived Picasso's passion for the arena. In the mid-1950s Picasso created the first of his celebrated bullfight posters using bright, festive colors (page 39).

In the 1955 poster Picasso offers us both the plan and elevation viewpoints: the circle of the arena and the structure of the roof (seen here as the dividing dark band between the figures) is presented to

us as an aerial view, while the bull, bullfighter, and audience are seen in profile as if being observed from the viewpoint of a spectator inside the arena. On one side of the arena in bright sunshine waits the bull, while in the shadow the bullfighter prepares with his banderillos.

The 1956 poster is a variation of the same composition, though slightly more complex (page 48). On the left waits the bull, which Picasso has provided with a large, all-seeing eye in profile. On the right the mounted picador on his horse waits in the doorway to the arena. The entire image has been placed within a circular containing-line, which acts as the walls to the bullring.

While in this poster we are awaiting the action of the bullfight, in a third poster made the following year in 1957, the action has reached the climax: the mounted picador is plunging his lance into the bull. Here the figures have been reduced to the minimum number of lines required for complete recognition. Simple yet effective, the figures are reminiscent of those which decorate Greek geometric vases of the ninth to the eighth centuries BC.

The influence of ancient art appears again in later bullfight posters, in particular in the poster from 1960. Here there are no horses, toreros, picadors or spectators, only bulls composed of simple outlines that to many are like the prehistoric cave paintings of bulls found at Altimira in Spain.

The poster that is often regarded as Picasso's finest linocut is the 1958 bullfight poster. Here the image is not of bulls but of the matador. In a manner reminiscent of his painting *Girl in a Mirror* (1932, Collection, The Museum of Modern Art, New York), Picasso presents us with two aspects of the same face. Constructed on the same plane are a full-frontal face and a face in profile. In the profile, the bun and pigtail of the matador's wig, his ear, eye, nose, mouth and chin can be seen. Yet the same eye, chin, nose and mouth are used to complete the structure of the front view of the face.

Even in connexion with an exhibition of Picasso's ceramics, in the poster commissioned by the town of Céret, the bullfight theme appears. The white ceramic plate at the center of the poster is decorated with the figures of men and women dancing the traditional Catalonian 'Sardana.' Yet Picasso's arrangements of the figures very subtly manages to suggest the outline of a bull. Whether this was intentional or not, it is worth noting that one of Céret's major industries was the training of bulls for the 'corrida.' A rather light-hearted touch is the manner in which Picasso has presented his own name, rather as though it is composed of flashing lightbulbs.

Further Spanish themes were developed in the posters for the Galeries Louise Leiris in 1960 and Henri Tranche in Paris in 1951. Both of these posters have been described as 'calligraphic,' as the hand-drawn lettering has the same qualities of

Left: Picasso's gouache *Head of a Faun* (1947), a motif which can be found throughout Picasso's oeuvre.

Below left: Picasso and friends at Antibes in 1937. On the far right is Dora Maar; in front sits Man Ray.

Right: Picasso in 1955 in his studio at the Villa La Californie.

Below: Picasso's vase from around 1947-48 in the shape of a woman is decorated with colored slips and incised surfaces.

Below right: Picasso in 1954 in front of one of his own posters. On the right stands the woman bullfighter Pierrette le Boudiec.

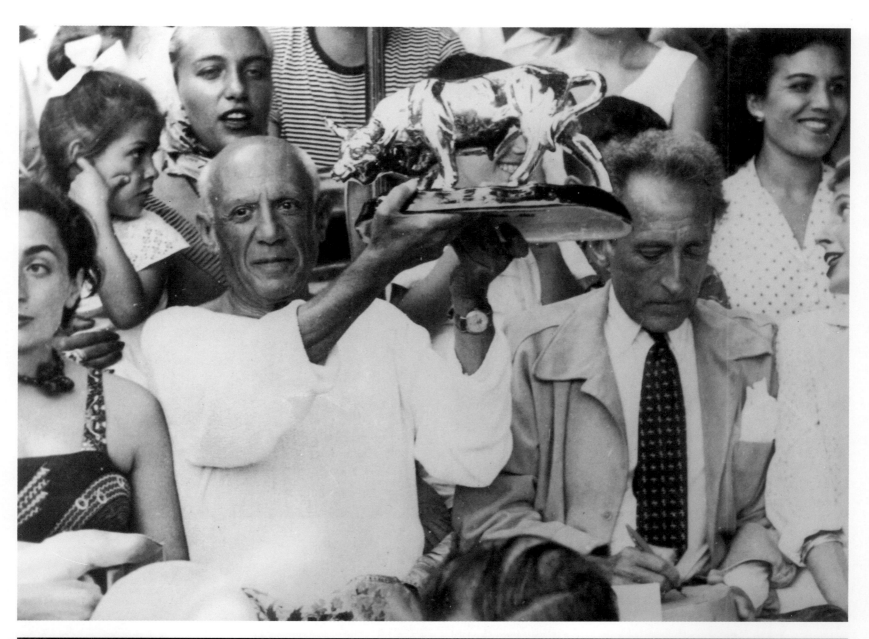

line as the drawing, with one line flowing naturally into the next. While the poster for Galerie Louise Leiris restates the theme of the mounted picador, the poster for the exhibition of Latin-American art depicts the popular figures from Cervantes' novel of Don Quixote and Sancho Panza. The economy of line is such that at the same time that Sancho Panza's hand is

holding a dove, it also makes up the dove's wing feathers. The same qualities of line can also be seen in the 'Manolo Huguet' poster of 1957 which invests the portrait of the bullfighter with a calm confidence and courage.

During this period in Vallauris Picasso also became very active in the peace movement. Having already expressed his

disgust and horror of war in the most famous of all his works *Guernica* in 1937, and later in *The Charnel House* (page 15) from 1945, which epitomizes Picasso's feelings concerning the disasters of World War II, Picasso turned his attention to proclaiming peace. A familiar sight on many of the posters is the symbol of the dove of peace, sometimes against the

background of a rainbow, at other times nesting on abandoned military hardware. In some posters flowers take the place of doves, some have hands grasping the stems to illustrate the elements of the brotherhood of man as a prerequisite for peace.

A variation of the peace theme is one poster designed in 1953 for an exhibition in Rome and later used for Picasso's vast *War and Peace* exhibition in Milan. This poster was designed to illustrate the section dealing with the horrors of war. A few simple heavy lines in red have been drawn against a dark background, and yet the position of the arm and face, the clenched hand and the wide eyes reveal all the anguish and pain of people caught in the horrors of war.

Top left: Picasso at the bull fight in 1955; to his left is Jean Cocteau.

Above left: Picasso speaking at the 1950 peace conference in Sheffield.

Above: *Girl Before a Mirror* (1932), oil on canvas.

19

In 1954 Picasso's relationship with Françoise Gilot came to an end. The previous year he had met Jacqueline Roque in Perpignan and the two were soon sharing the Paris studio in the rue des Grands Augustines. They were finally married in 1958, and despite an age difference of over forty-five years, Picasso's relationship with Jacqueline would endure for the rest of his life that is until he died at the age of 91 in 1973.

Like Françoise's before her, the image of Jacqueline also appears in Picasso's posters. Her profile is to be seen in several works where Picasso utilized his characteristic treatment of line. In the 1960

poster, the subjects that interested him throughout his life appear once again. Although the poster was designed to advertise an exhibition of Picasso's graphic works at the Galerie des Ponchettes in Nice, it is decorated with symbols of Spain. Jacqueline appears in profile, appearing as a 'señorita,' dressed in the traditional Spanish costume of a mantilla and fan, standing on a balcony overlooking the arena wherein the torero faces the bull. The economy of line is such that Picasso has been able to suggest a small dog standing at Jacqueline's feet. The dog has in fact been formed out of the wavy line that also serves to suggest a

second tier or ruffle on Jacqueline's dress.

The year 1954 appears to have been a turning point for Picasso in many ways. The same year brought news of the death of his old friend and artistic rival, Henri Matisse. Of him, Picasso had often said: 'Au fond il n'y a que Matisse' (All things considered, there is only Matisse). In addition to some posters that bear witness to the influences of Matisse, such as the 1956 Vallauris exhibition poster (page 45) with its simple areas of color, and the 1962 poster for the linocut exhibition in Baden-Baden which is reminiscent of Matisse's later work involving cut paper, it has often been said that Matisse's death

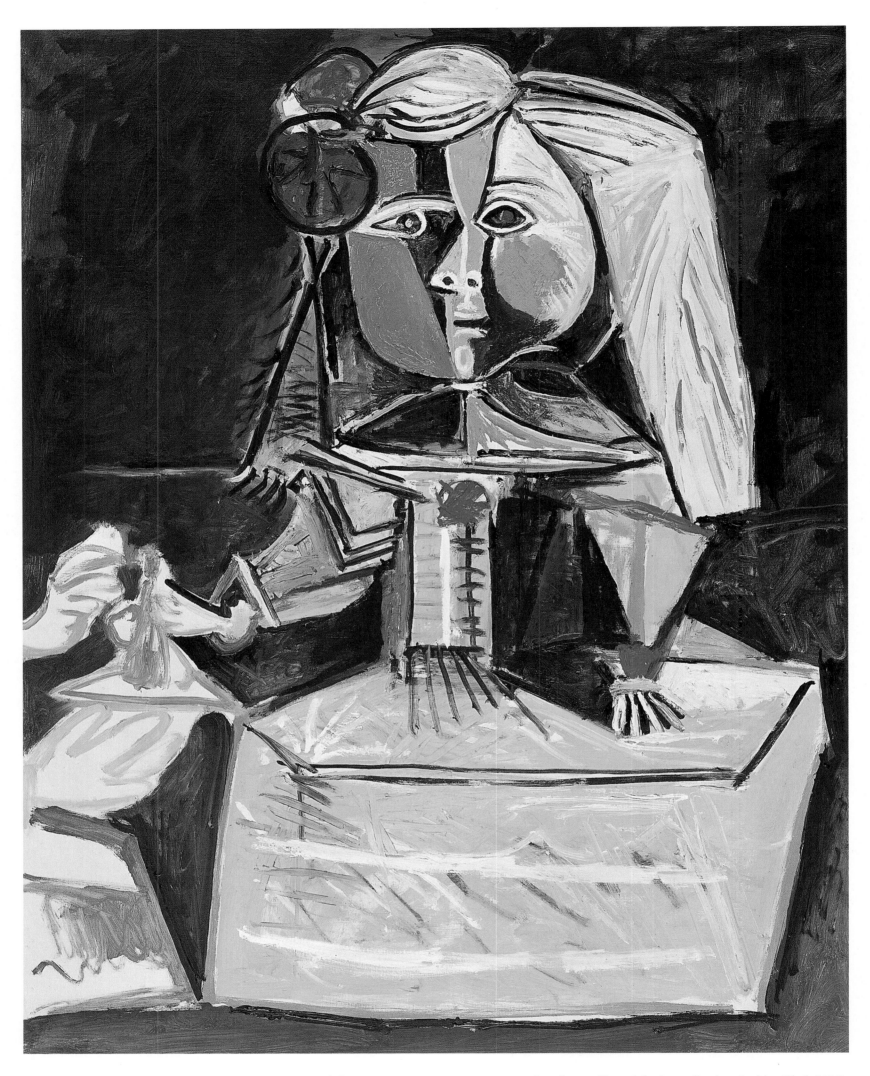

was the driving force behind Picasso's cycle of variations of Old Master paintings.

Between December 1954 and February 1955 Picasso completed a series of fifteen variations on Eugène Delacroix's *Women of Algiers in their Apartment*, a theme which Matisse had also reworked in his *Odalisque* paintings. Picasso's cycle of paintings produced a wide variety of colors and compositions. Starting with recognizable forms, the paintings progress to a state close to abstract monochromes.

This was not the first time Picasso had used other painters' works as the basis for

Above left: *Jacqueline in a Rocking Chair* (1954) shows Jacqueline Roque, Picasso's last wife, whose image frequently appears in Picasso's paintings and posters.

Above: *The Infanta Margarita* (1957) one of a series of works inspired by Velázquez's *Las Meninas*.

compositions according to his own terms. Previous examples come from a variety of sources like Le Nain, Renoir, Poussin, Cranach, Courbet and El Greco. Nor would the re-working of Delacroix's themes be the last. The major cycle of works based on Manet's *Déjeuner sur l'Herbe* resulted in 27 paintings, 140 drawings, 3 linocuts, and 10 cardboard maquettes for sculptures as well as the 1962 poster advertising the exhibition of '*Déjeuner*–inspired' works at the Galerie Madoura in Cannes.

Picasso also re-worked the themes of the *Fêtes Galantes* of Watteau, such as in the 1957 poster for Galerie Louise Leiris which depicts two men shaking tambourines while between them stands the figure of a girl whose hands they hold. The drawing technique in this poster, which can also be seen in the 1961 Sala Gaspar poster, is characteristic of some of Picasso's work from the 1930s, in particular, the series of etchings and aquatints for *The Dream and Lie of Franco* (1937). These prints were originally produced for a pamphlet but were later produced as postcards which were sold to raise money for the Republican cause during the Spanish Civil War.

Following the split with Françoise, Picasso and Jacqueline moved to the Villa Californie overlooking the sea at Cannes. Here in the autumn of 1958 Picasso embarked on a concentrated period of work and in the space of two months completed a series of variations on *Las Meninas* by Velázquez.

Picasso had admired the original painting ever since he had first visited Madrid and the Prado museum with his father in 1895. In his own way, Picasso reworked Velázquez's painting: throughout the series of 58 paintings Picasso transformed the lighting from the dark somberness of the Spanish Royal Court into the bright sunshine of the French Riviera and placed figures in different positions, altering their gestures and the textures of their clothes.

The first of the paintings is the largest and the most complete of the whole series, while the paintings that followed concentrated on details, groups of figures, individuals and finally, towards the end of the cycle, a portrait of Jacqueline. All of these motifs were to be taken up again in later posters advertising Picasso's exhibitions.

Of the 58 paintings based on *Las Meninas*, 14 works deal with a secondary theme of the action 'behind the scenes'. Velázquez had painted himself painting the King and Queen, who in the painting appear only in the reflexion of a small mirror. The 'behind-the-scenes' element in the creation of the painting appealed to Picasso which in his own variations is manifested by a series of observations of his own immediate surroundings – the studio, the balcony, and the doves which nested on it, the view through the open studio window of the sea and nearby islands and palm trees.

The simple compositions, harmonious colors and attractive themes of the portraits and balcony scenes also translated perfectly into lithographs for posters regardless of whether they advertised Picasso's exhibitions or the beauty of the Côte d'Azur.

It is evident that in his posters, as in every medium in which he worked, Picasso was equally as inventive and original. Although there are instances where techniques, approaches, motifs, or details are repeated, no two posters by Picasso are ever alike. Furthermore, Picasso's posters also stand as fine examples of his creative range and ability.

Left: *Women of Algiers (After Delacroix)* (1955), one of a series of 15 variations on the theme of the odalisque.

Above: *Las Meninas (The Doves I)*, one of 14 of Picasso's 'behind-the-scenes' paintings of his studio, the balcony, and nesting doves.

BALLETS RUSSES
DE DIAGHILEW
1909 - 1929

MARS - AVRIL 1939

MUSÉE DES ARTS DÉCORATIFS
Palais du Louvre _ Pavillon de Marsan, 107, rue de Rivoli

ENTRÉE 6 FRANCS

Ballets Russes de Diaghilev,
1939
Exhibition poster for The Museum of
Decorative Arts, Paris
Lithograph
23⅝×15¾ inches (60×40 cm)
Edition: 500
Private Collection

Pottery-Flowers-Perfume, 1948
Vallauris exhibition poster
Lithograph
23⅞×15¾ inches (60.5×40 cm)
Edition: 118
Private Collection

Pottery-Flowers-Perfume, 1948
Vallauris exhibition poster
Lithograph
23⅞×15¾ inches (60.5×40 cm)
Edition: 300 and 25 in black, signed and
numbered; 24 in color, signed and
numbered
Private Collection

Pottery-Flowers-Perfume, 1948
Vallauris exhibition poster
Lithograph
24×15¾ inches (61×40 cm)
Edition: 300 and 25 in black, signed and
numbered; 25 in color, signed and
numbered
Private Collection

LITHOGRAPHIES
de
PABLO PICASSO
pour
LE CHANT DES MORTS
de
PIERRE REVERDY
TÉRIADE ÉDITEUR

EXPOSITION
chez
LOUIS CARRÉ
10, Avenue de Messine, Paris-8ᵉ
DU 17 AU 31 DÉCEMBRE 1948

VALLAURIS

L'HOMME AU MOUTON DE PICASSO

EXPOSITION
POTERIES
ART ET TECHNIQUE

29 JUILLET - 15 SEPTEMBRE 1950

MOURLOT - PARIS

'The Song of the Dead', 1948
Exhibition poster, lithograph
25⅝×18⅛ inches (65×46 cm)
Private Collection

Vallauris: 'L'Homme au Mouton' by Picasso, 1950
Exhibition poster, lithograph
24½×18⅞ inches (62×43 cm)
Private Collection

EXPOSITION HISPANO-
AMERICAINE
30 NOVEMBRE
22 DECEMBRE
1951
PARIS
GALERIE
HENRI TRONCHE
6 AV. PERCIER

Latin-American Show, 1951
Exhibition poster for Galerie Henri
Tronche, Paris
Lithograph
25⅝×19⅝ inches (65×50 cm)
Edition: 300 and 100 signed by the
artist.
Private Collection

Vallauris Exhibition, 1951
25⅝×19¾ inches (64.5×50.2 cm)
Edition: 400 in brown and white on
vellum; 400 in green on vellum
The Metropolitan Museum of Art, New
York; The Mr and Mrs Charles Kramer
Collection; Gift of Mr and Mrs Charles
Kramer, 1979

Vallauris Exhibition, 1952
Linocut poster
31½×23⅝ inches (80×60 cm)
Edition: 450 in black on white paper;
350 in black on yellow paper; 500 in
black on orange paper; 500 in green on
yellow paper; 100 artist's impressions in
green on yellow paper

The Metropolitan Museum of Art, New
York; The Mr and Mrs Charles Kramer
Collection; Gift of Mr and Mrs Charles
Kramer, 1979

**Picasso: 200 works from 1920
to 1953,** 1953
Exhibition poster for National Gallery
of Modern Art, Rome
Offset lithograph
39⅜×27½ inches (100×70 cm)
Edition: unknown size
Private Collection

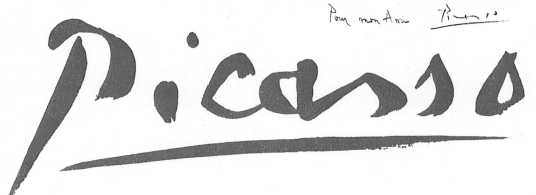

200 OPERE DAL 1920 AL 1953

GALLERIA NAZIONALE D'ARTE MODERNA

ROMA - VALLE GIULIA MAGGIO GIUGNO 1953

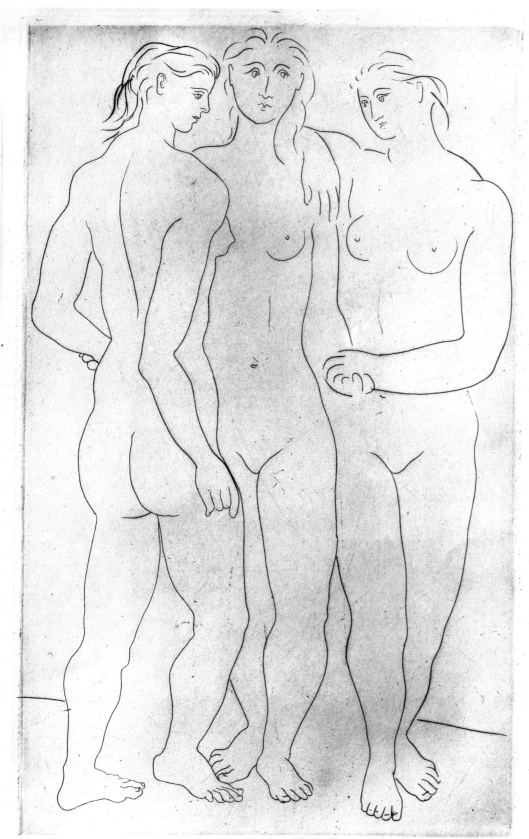

17/100 Picasso

Vallauris Exhibition, 1953
Color typographic poster
2 sizes: 26¾×20½ inches (68×52 cm)
and 31⅞×23¼ inches (81×59 cm)
Edition: 2000
Private Collection

The Three Graces II, 1922-23
Etching
12¾×7¾ inches (32.5×19.7cm)
Edition: 100
Courtesy of the Trustees of the Victoria
and Albert Museum, London

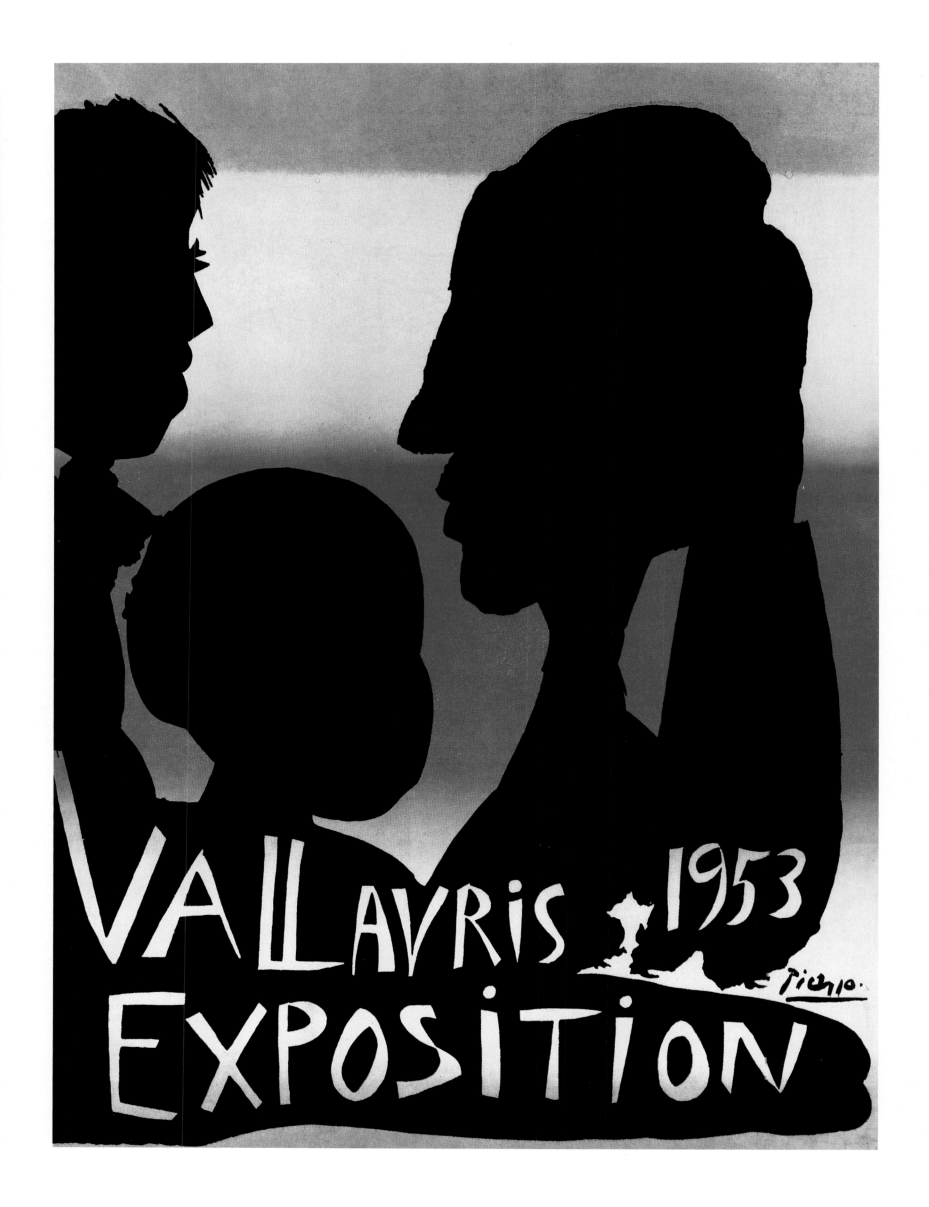

Vallauris Exhibition, 1954
Linocut poster
27½×22¾ inches (69.9×57.8 cm)
Edition: 600
The Metropolitan Museum of Art, New
York; The Mr and Mrs Charles Kramer
Collection; Gift of Mr and Mrs Charles
Kramer, 1979

Prague Spring, 1954
Offset lithograph
Poster design conceived by Jarmila
Maranova
39⅜×27½ inches (100×70 cm)
Edition: 200
Private Collection

PRAŽSKÉ JARO

Painter with Model Knitting,
1927
Etching
7⅝×11 inches (28×19.4 cm)
Courtesy of the Trustees of the Victoria
and Albert Museum, London

Bulls in Vallauris, 1955
Linocut poster
35×23⅜ inches (88.9×59.4 cm)
Edition: 200
The Metropolitan Museum of Art, New
York; The Mr and Mrs Charles Kramer
Collection; Gift of Mr and Mrs Charles
Kramer, 1979

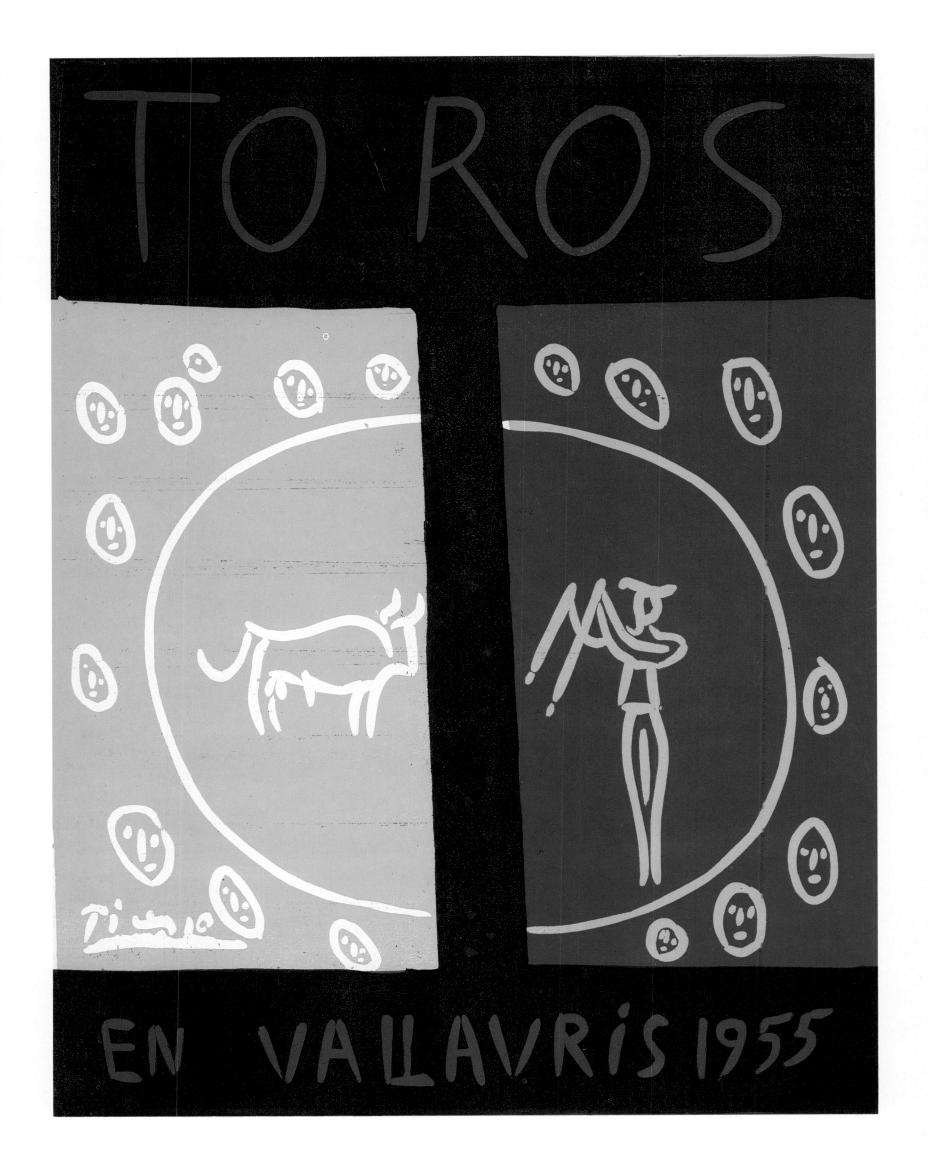

Deucalion and Pyrrha, 1930
From Ovid's *Metamorphoses*
12¼×8⅞ inches (31.2×22.4 cm)
Courtesy of the Trustees of the Victoria
and Albert Museum, London

Vallauris Exhibition, 1955
Linocut poster
31⅜×23½ inches (59.7×39.7 cm)
Edition: 600
The Metropolitan Museum of Art, New
York; The Mr and Mrs Charles Kramer
Collection; Gift of Mr and Mrs Charles
Kramer, 1979

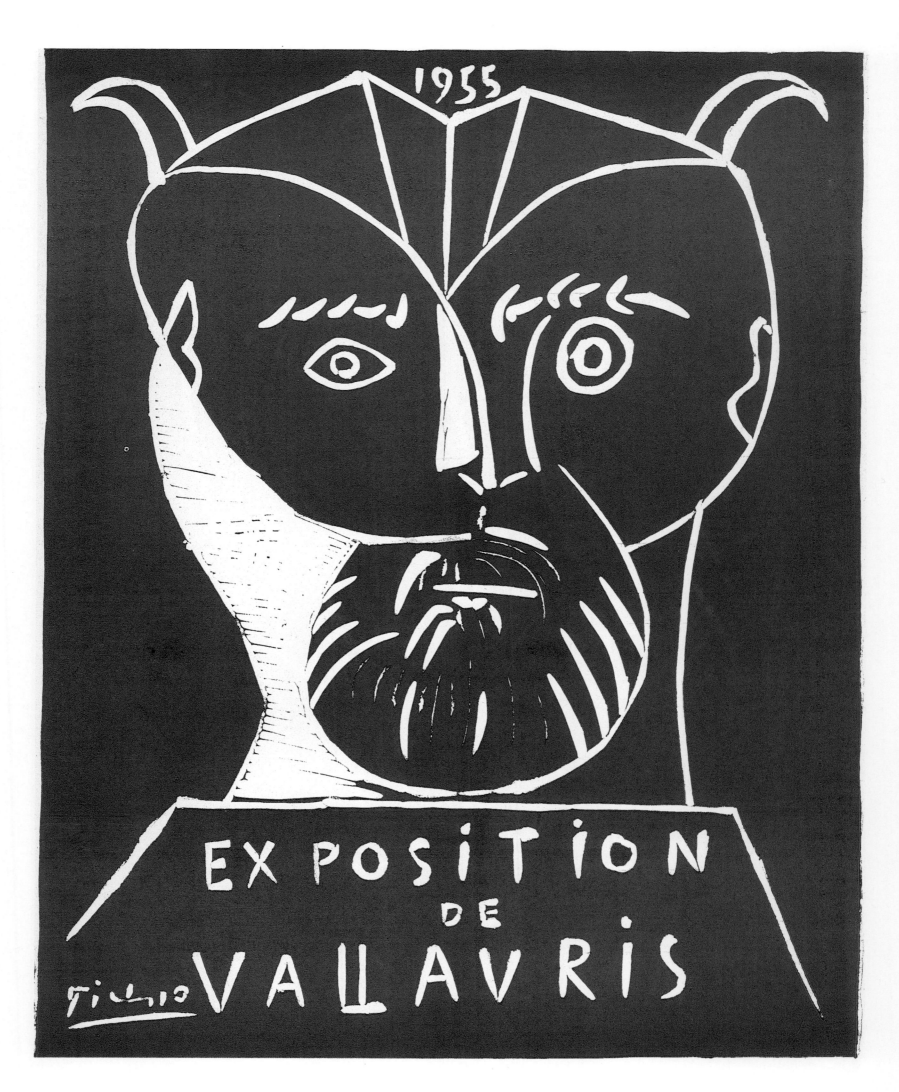

Vallauris Exhibition, 1955
Linocut poster
The Metropolitan Museum of Art, New
York; The Mr and Mrs Charles Kramer
Collection; Gift of Mr and Mrs Charles
Kramer, 1979

Vallauris Exhibition, 1955
Linocut poster
33¼×23⅛ inches (84.5×58.7 cm)
Edition: 600
The Metropolitan Museum of Art, New
York; The Mr and Mrs Charles Kramer
Collection; Gift of Mr and Mrs Charles
Kramer, 1979

Minotaur, Drinker, and
Women, 1933
From the *Vollard Suite*
Etching
11¼×14⅜ inches
Courtesy of the Trustees of the Victoria
and Albert Museum, London

Vallauris Exhibition, 1956
Linocut poster
39⅜×25⅞ inches (100×65.7 cm)
Edition: 200
The Metropolitan Museum of Art, New
York; The Mr and Mrs Charles Kramer
Collection; Gift of Mr and Mrs Charles
Kramer, 1979

46

Bulls in Vallauris, 1956
Linocut poster
39¼×25⅞ inches (99.7×65.7 cm)
Edition: 200
The Metropolitan Museum of Art, New
York; The Mr and Mrs Charles Kramer
Collection; Gift of Mr and Mrs Charles
Kramer, 1979

Minotaur, 1935
Etching
19⅝×27¼ inches (49.8×69.3 cm)
Museo Picasso, Barcelona

50

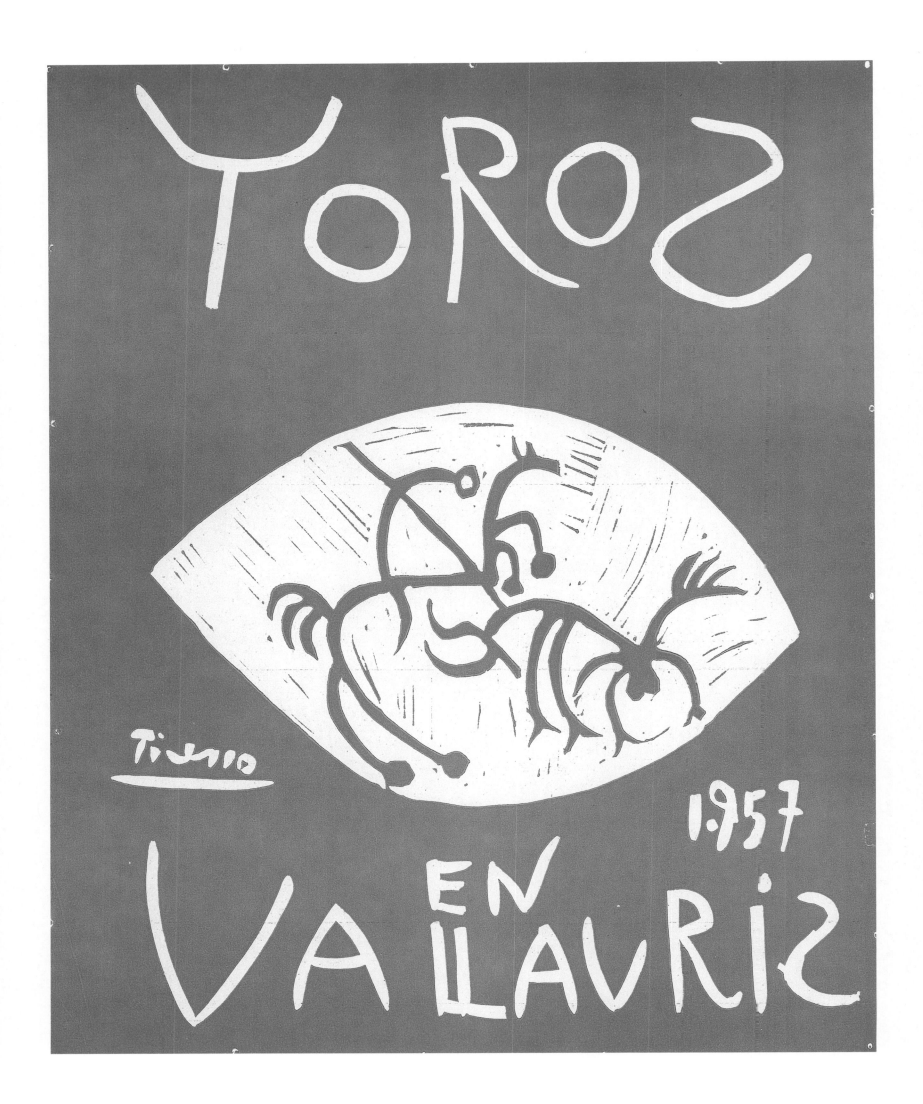

Galerie 65, Cannes, 1956
Lithograph
27½×18⅞ inches (70×48 cm)
Edition: 2000 and 100 signed and
numbered
Private Collection

Bulls in Vallauris, 1957
Linocut poster
31⅞×25½ inches (81×64.8 cm)
Edition: 198
The Metropolitan Museum of Art, New
York; The Mr and Mrs Charles Kramer
Collection; Gift of Mr and Mrs Charles
Kramer, 1979

51

L'Aveille, 1941-42
From Buffon's *Histoire Naturelle*
Etching
14⅛×11 inches (36×28 cm)
Courtesy of the Trustees of the Victoria
and Albert Museum, London

Vallauris Exhibition, 1957
Linocut poster
39⅜×26½ inches (100×67.3 cm)
Edition: 175
The Metropolitan Museum of Art, New
York; The Mr and Mrs Charles Kramer
Collection; Gift of Mr and Mrs Charles
Kramer, 1979

Picasso Paintings 1955-56, 1957
Exhibition poster for Galerie Leiris
Lithograph
29½×21¼ inches (75×54 cm)
Edition: 1500 and 25 artist's proofs
Private Collection

La Santerelle, 1941-42
From Buffon's _Histoire Naturelle_
Etching
14⅛×11 inches (36×28 cm)
Courtesy of the Trustees of the Victoria
and Albert Museum, London

Illustration inédite de Picasso

Dans

l'ARGILE

de

PICASSO

Poèmes de *Henri-Dante Alberti*

Dans l'Argile de Picasso, 1957
Lithograph
Edition: 200
Private Collection

The Dragonfly, 1941-42
From Buffon's *Histoire Naturelle*
Etching
14⅛×11 inches (36×28 cm)
Courtesy of the Trustees of the Victoria
and Albert Museum, London

57

MUSÉE D'ART MODERNE
CÉRET
AOUT - SEPTEMBRE - OCTOBRE 1957

MOURLOT IMP.

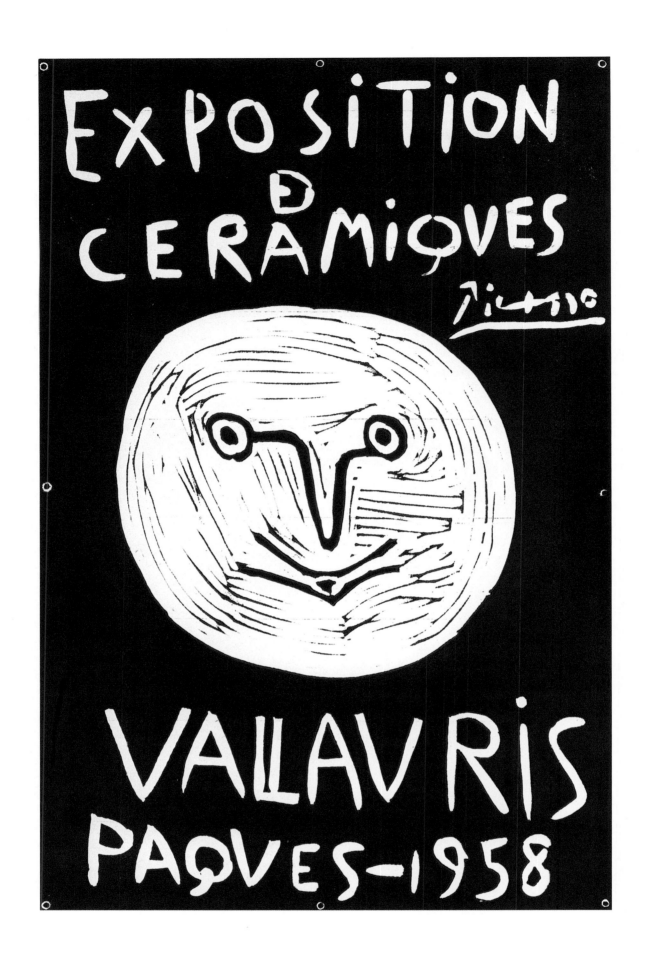

EXPOSITION ⊖ CERAMIQUES

Picasso

VALLAURIS PAQVES-1958

Manolo Huguet, 1957
Exhibition poster for the Museum of
Modern Art, Céret
Lithograph
30⅓×20⅞ inches (77×53 cm)
Edition: 500 and 100 proofs signed and
numbered by the artist, some hand-
colored using crayon
Private Collection

Vallauris Ceramics
Exhibition, 1958
Linocut poster
24¼×17⅜ inches (66.7×41.1 cm)
Edition: 100 and 200 printed on offset
vellum
The Metropolitan Museum of Art, New
York; The Mr and Mrs Charles Kramer
Collection; Gift of Mr and Mrs Charles
Kramer, 1979

Maison de la Pensée Française
2 Rue de l'Elysée
Exposition de Céramiques
du 8 mars au 30 juin
PICASSO

Maison de la Pensée Française,
2 Rue de L'Elysée

Exposition de Céramiques
du 8 mars au 30 juin

PICASSO

Picasso
6.14.1.58.

Previous pages, left:

Picasso Ceramics Exhibition,
1958
Exhibition poster for the Maison de la
Pensée Française, Paris
Lithograph
25⅝×18⅞ inches (65×48 cm)
Edition: 500
Private Collection

Previous pages, right:

Picasso Ceramics Exhibition,
1958
Exhibition poster for the Maison de la
Pensée Française, Paris
Lithograph
25⅝×18¾ inches (65×47.5 cm)
Edition: 500
Private Collection

Bulls in Vallauris, 1958
Linocut poster
36¾×29½ inches (93.3×74.9 cm)
Edition: 195
The Metropolitan Museum of Art, New
York; The Mr and Mrs Charles Kramer
Collection; Gift of Mr and Mrs Charles
Kramer, 1979

The Minotaur, 1958
Oil on canvas
Mayor Gallery, London

63

The Cat, 1941-42
From Buffon's *Histoire Naturelle*
Etching
14⅛×11 inches (36×28 cm)
Courtesy of the Trustees of the Victoria
and Albert Museum, London

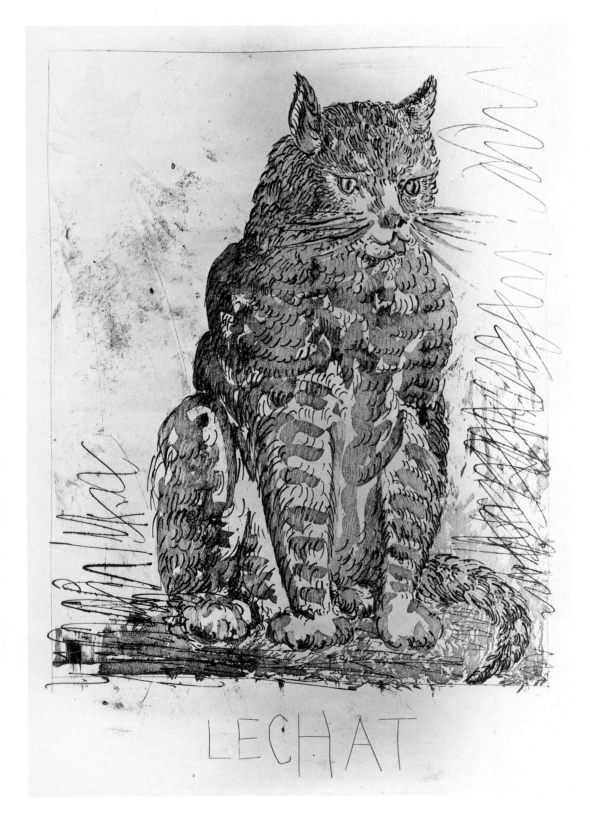

VALLAVRIS

dix ans de céramique
de
PiCASSO
plus
100 potiers - oeuvres
récentes

Hall Nérolium
19 juillet - 28 Septembre

Picasso: Ceramics and White Pottery Exhibition, 1958
Linocut poster
26×19⅜ inches (66×49.2 cm)
Edition: 875 and 125 impressions
printed on Arches paper
The Metropolitan Museum of Art, New York; The Mr and Mrs Charles Kramer Collection; Gift of Mr and Mrs Charles Kramer, 1979

LA BICHE

The Doe, 1941-42
From Buffon's *Histoire Naturelle*
Etching
14⅛×11 inches (36×28 cm)
Courtesy of the Trustees of the Victoria and Albert Museum, London

66

Vallauris Exhibition, 1958
Linocut poster
39⅜×25½ inches (100×64.8 cm)
Edition: 175 and 100 impressions printed
on offset vellum and 25 artist's
impressions
The Metropolitan Museum of Art, New
York; The Mr and Mrs Charles Kramer
Collection; Gift of Mr and Mrs Charles
Kramer, 1979

The Goldfinch, 1941-42
From Buffon's *Histoire Naturelle*
Etching
14⅛×11 inches (36×28 cm)
Courtesy of the Trustees of the Victoria
and Albert Museum, London

69

***Original Posters by Masters of
the Paris School,*** 1959
Exhibition poster for the Maison de la
Pensée Française, Paris
Lithograph
26×19¼ inches (66×49 cm)
Edition: 1000
Private Collection

Round of Friendship, 1959
Color lithograph
Museo de la Abadia, Monserrat,
Catalonia

AFFICHES
ORIGINALES
DES Maîtres de l'Ecole
de PARIS
Maison de la Pensée Française
2 rue de l'Elysée PARIS
à partir du 27 Juin 1959.
Picasso
10.6.59.

Women and Goat, 1959
Color linocut
20⅞×25¼ inches (53×64 cm)
Edition: 50
Private Collection

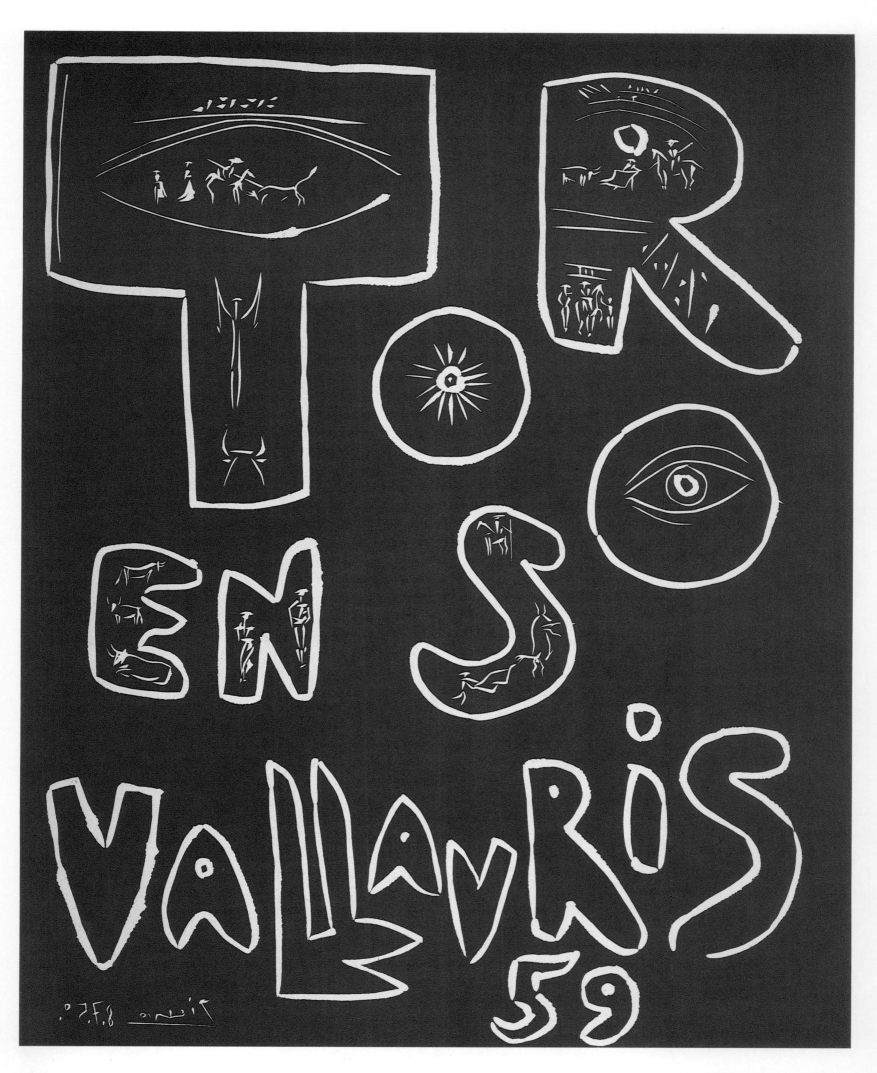

Bulls in Vallauris, 1959
30⅛×22¼ inches (76.5×56.5 cm)
Edition: 190 and 25 impressions 'hors commerce' and 25 artist's proofs
The Metropolitan Museum of Art, New York; The Mr and Mrs Charles Kramer Collection; Gift of Mr and Mrs Charles Kramer, 1979

Picasso: Printed Works, 1959
Exhibition poster for Galerie des Ponchettes, Nice
Lithograph
26×19⅞ inches (66×50.5 cm)
Edition: 625 and 145 signed and 15 reserved by the artist
Private Collection

**Vallauris Ceramics
Exhibition,** 1959
30×22¼ inches (76.5×56.5 cm)
Edition: 175 signed and numbered; 120
unsigned and un-numbered; 25 artist's
proofs; The Metropolitan Museum of
Art, New York; The Mr and Mrs
Charles Kramer Collection; Gift of Mr
and Mrs Charles Kramer, 1979

Peace, 1960
Poster for the Peace Movement
Lithograph
47¼×31⅝ inches (120×80.5 cm)
Edition: 25,000 and 1000 signed on the
litho plate, 200 impressions numbered
and signed by the artist
Private Collection

PAIX
DÉSARMEMENT
POUR LE SUCCÈS
DE LA
CONFÉRENCE AU SOMMET
PARIS, MAI 1960
LE MOUVEMENT DE LA PAIX

Vallauris Exhibition, 1960
Linocut poster
29⅝×24 inches (75.2×61.2 cm)
Edition: 170
The Metropolitan Museum of Art, New
York; The Mr and Mrs Charles Kramer
Collection; Gift of Mr and Mrs Charles
Kramer, 1979

Bulls in Vallauris, 1960
Linocut poster
29⅝×24⅝ inches (75.2×62.5 cm)
Edition: 185 and 237 unsigned and un-
numbered.
The Metropolitan Museum of Art, New
York; The Mr and Mrs Charles Kramer
Collection; Gift of Mr and Mrs Charles
Kramer, 1979

Picasso: Drawings 1959-60,
1960
Lithograph
26×19⅝ inches (66×50 cm)
Private Collection

Picasso Drawings, 1961
Lithograph
35½×25⅝ inches (90×65 cm)
Edition: 560
Private Collection

LECRAFAUD

Vallauris Exhibition, 1961
Linocut poster
29½×24½ inches (74.9×62.2 cm)
Edition: 175 and 120 impressions 'hors
comerce' and 35 artist's proofs
The Metropolitan Museum of Art, New
York; The Mr and Mrs Charles Kramer
Collection; Gift of Mr and Mrs Charles
Kramer, 1979

The Toad, 1941-42
From Buffon's *Histoire Naturelle*
Etching
14⅛×11 inches (36×28 cm)
Courtesy of the Trustees of the Victoria
and Albert Museum, London

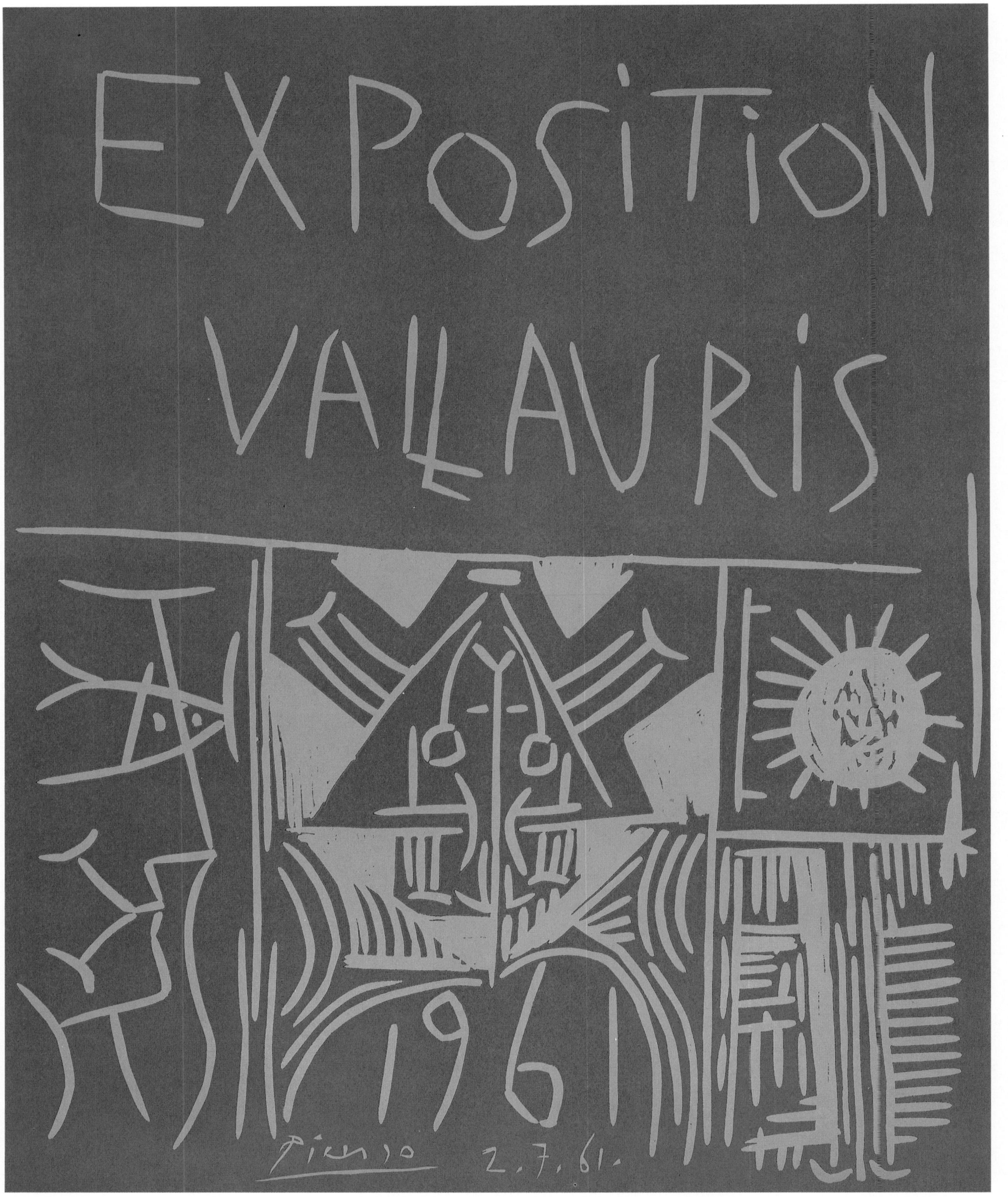
EXPOSITION
VALLAURIS
1961
Picasso 2.7.61.

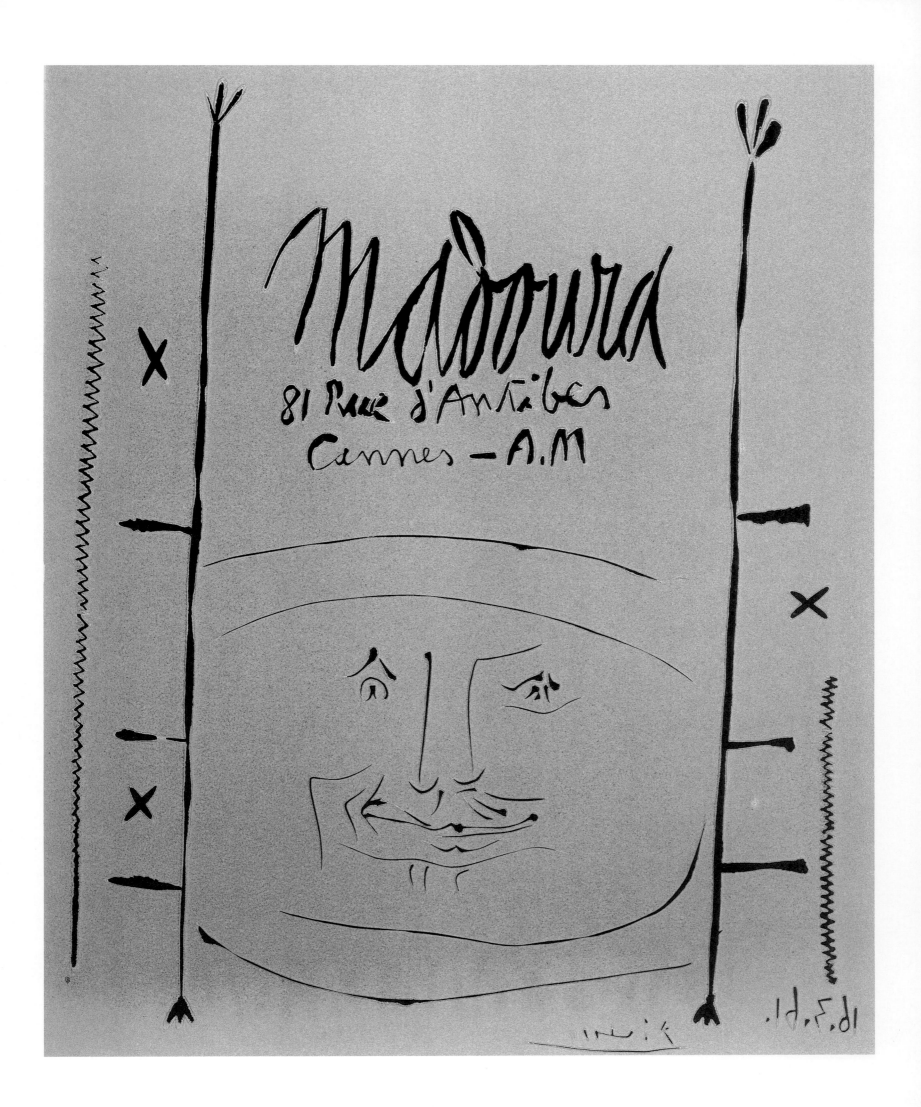

Gallery Madoura, Cannes, Exhibition, 1961
Linocut poster
29⅝×24½ inches (75.2×62.2 cm)
Edition: 100
The Metropolitan Museum of Art, New York; The Mr and Mrs Charles Kramer Collection; Gift of Mr and Mrs Charles Kramer, 1979

The Circus, 1945
Lithograph, second state
11½×19⅝ inches (29×50 cm)
Courtesy of the Trustees of the Victoria and Albert Museum, London

85

**Madoura Exhibition
Invitation,** 1961
Linocut
4⅜×9⅛ inches (11.1×23.2 cm)
Edition: 100
The Metropolitan Museum of Art, New
York; The Mr and Mrs Charles Kramer
Collection; Gift of Mr and Mrs Charles
Kramer, 1979

"BONNE FÊTE" MONSIEUR PICASSO
25 OCTOBER - 12 NOVEMBER 1961

For U.C.L.A.
picasso
23.5.61.

PICASSO

SELECTED FROM SOUTHERN CALIFORNIA COLLECTIONS
PRESENTED BY
THE UCLA ART COUNCIL
AT THE
UCLA ART GALLERIES
LOS ANGELES, CALIFORNIA

PRINTED IN FRANCE, BY MOURLOT

88

ALEX Maguy Galerie
de L'Elysée
69 r du fg
St Honoré
15.4.62.
Expose 7 Tableaux Majeurs
30 mai — 30 juin 62.

Previous pages, left:

'Bonne Fête' Monsieur Picasso, 1961
Exhibition poster for UCLA Art
Council at the UCLA Art Galleries,
University of California
Lithograph
27×25 inches (98.5×63.5 cm)
Edition: 2500 and 100 signed lithographs
Private Collection

Previous pages, right:

Alex Maguy Expose Sept Tableaux Majeurs, 1962
Exhibition poster for Galerie de
l'Elysee, Paris
Lithograph
25¾×19 inches (65.5×48.5 cm)
Edition: 1000
Private Collection

Right:

Peace, 1962
Poster for the World Congress for
Disarmament and Peace (Arabic text;
versions produced in various languages)
Photolithograph
39⅜×26 inches (100×66 cm)
Edition: 8000
Private Collection

Still Life under a Lamp, 1962
Color linocut
64×53 cm (25¼×20⅞ inches)
Edition: 50
Christie's, London

Côte d'Azur

Picasso

Côte d'Azur: Picasso, 1962
Lithograph
39⅜×26 inches (100×66.5 cm)
Edition: 15,000 impressions (one version
with text 'Cannes,' another with text
'Côte d'Azur'. Some artist's proofs
taken before lettering
Private Collection

The Butterfly, 1941–42
From Buffon's *Histoire Naturelle*
Etching
14⅛×11 inches (36×28 cm)
Courtesy of the Trustees of the Victoria
and Albert Museum, London

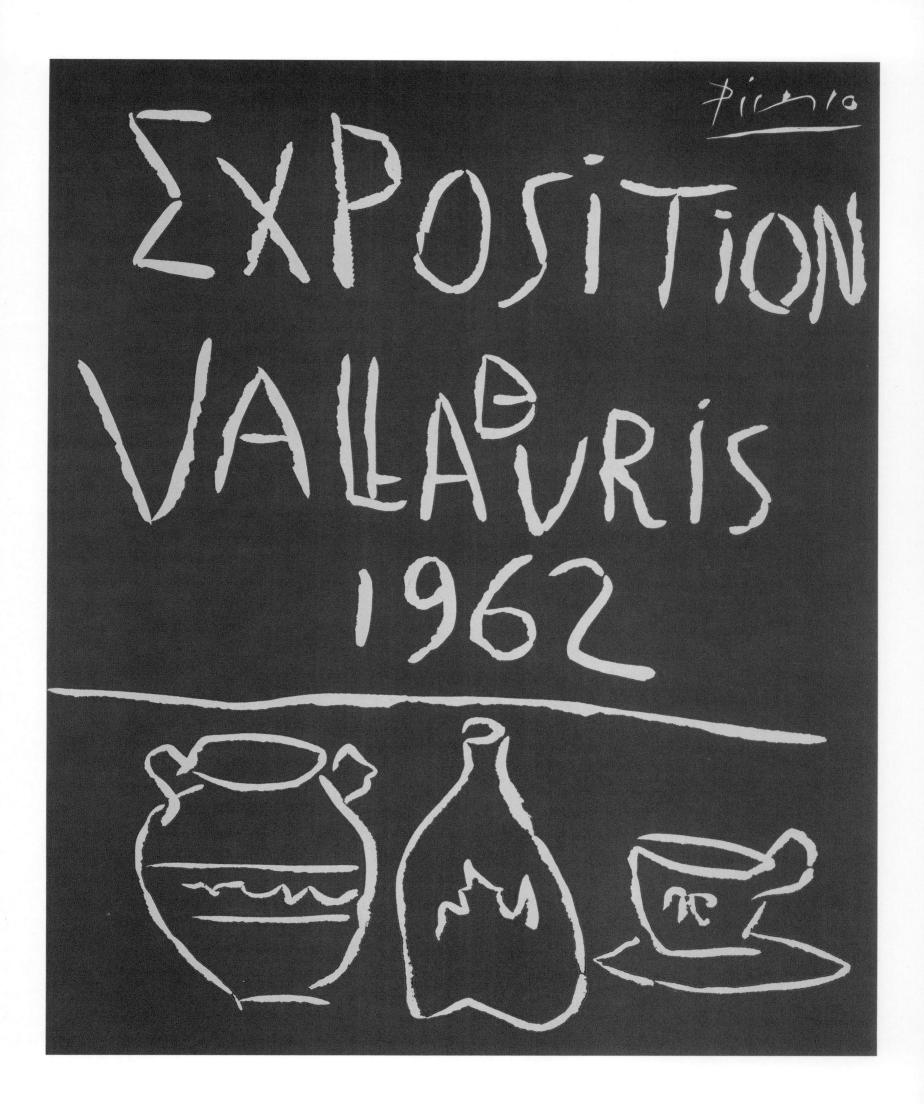

Vallauris Exhibition, 1962
Linocut poster
29½×24½ inches (74.9×62.2 cm)
Edition: 175
The Metropolitan Museum of Art, New
York; The Mr and Mrs Charles Kramer
Collection; Gift of Mr and Mrs Charles
Kramer, 1979

Picasso: Linocuts, 1962
Exhibition poster for Kunsthalle,
Baden-Baden
Color typographic poster
23½×16½ inches (59.5×42 cm)
Edition: 300
Private Collection

picasso **1958-1960** linolschnitte
Gesellschaft der Freunde junger Kunst Baden-Baden
in der Kunsthalle Baden-Baden 9. Mai -27. Mai 1962

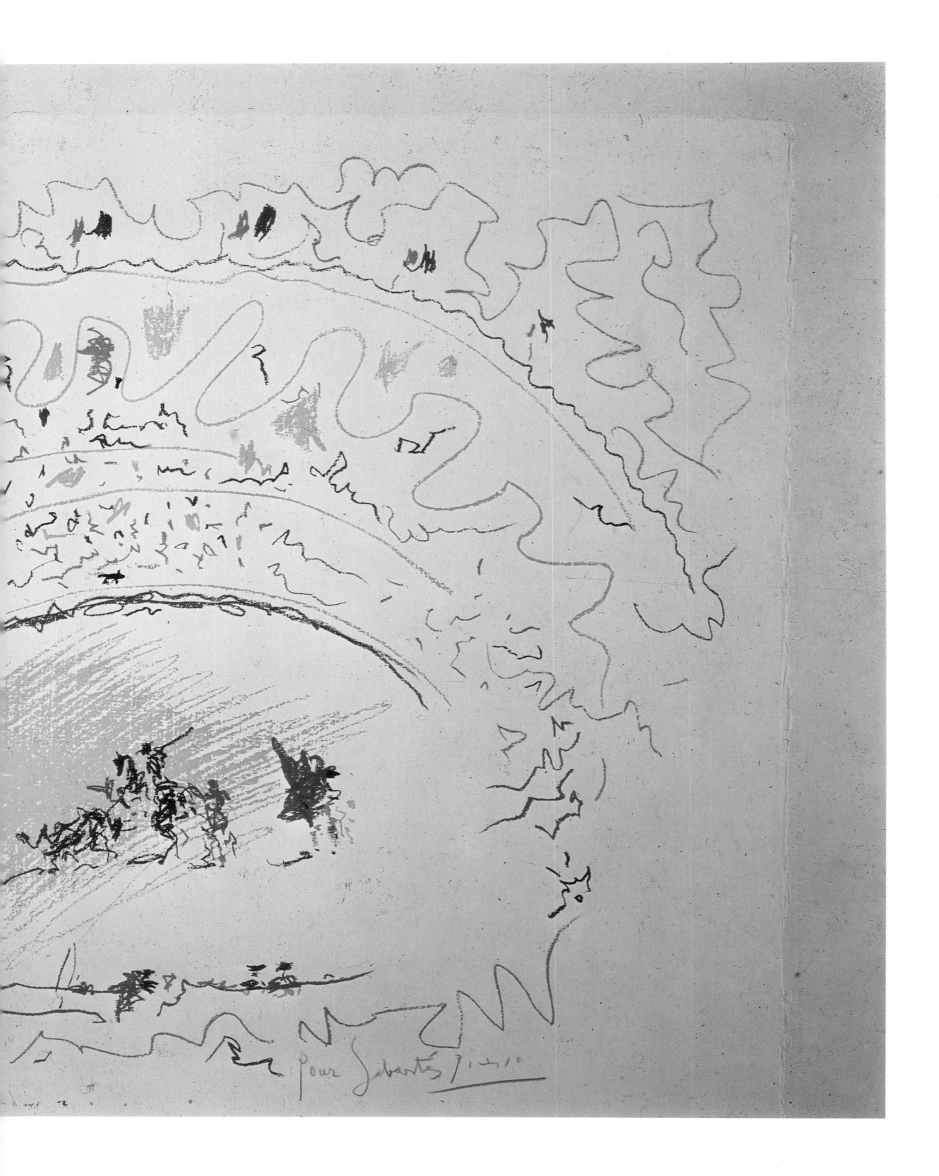

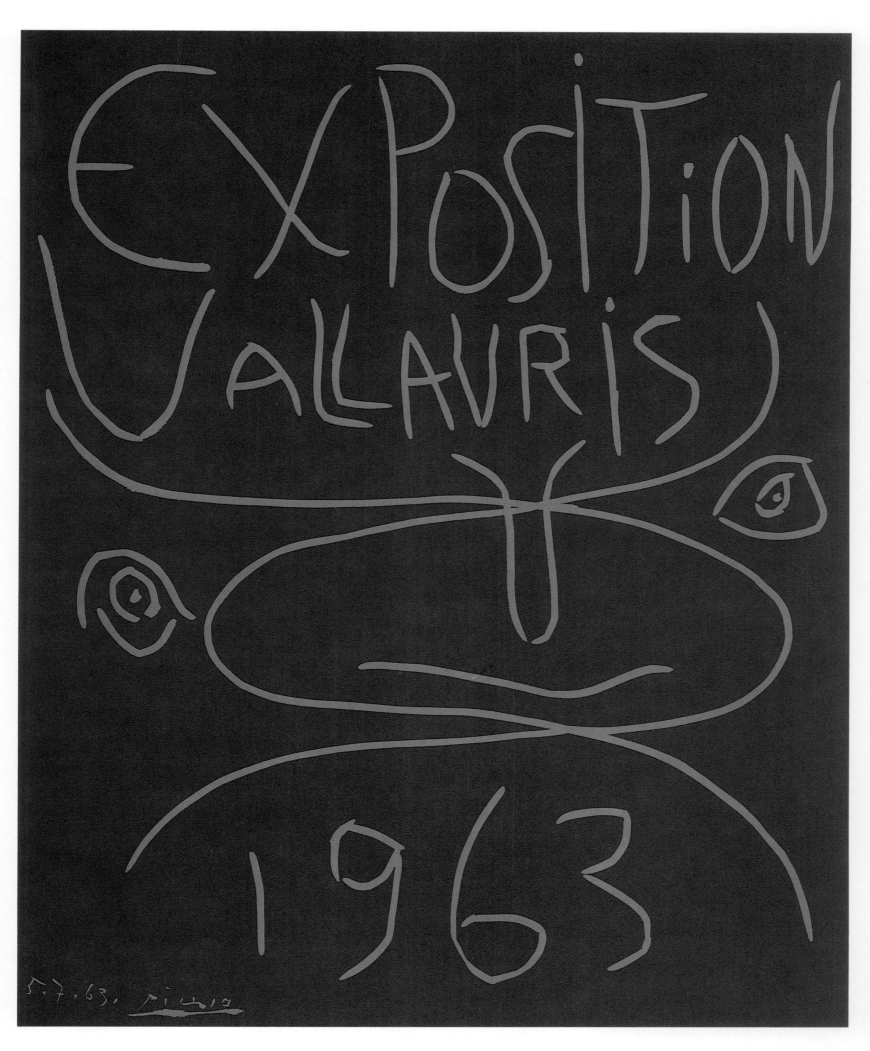

Vallauris Exhibition, 1963
Linocut poster
29⅝×24½ inches (75.2×62.2 cm)
Edition: 170
The Metropolitan Museum of Art, New
York; The Mr and Mrs Charles Kramer
Collection; Gift of Mr and Mrs Charles
Kramer, 1979

Picasso's 'Les Dejeuners':
Original Drawings, 1962
Exhibition poster for Galerie Madoura,
Cannes
Color typographic poster
20½×14¾ inches (52×37.5 cm)
Edition: 1025 and 75 signed, without
text
Private Collection

PICASSO
LES DÉJEUNERS

DESSINS ORIGINAUX DE PICASSO

GALERIE MADOURA

81 RUE D'ANTIBES - CANNES

A PARTIR DU 4 AOUT 1962

The Spanish Bull, 1941-42
From Buffon's *Histoire Naturelle*
Etching
14⅛×11 inches (36×28 cm)
Courtesy of the Trustees of the Victoria
and Albert Museum, London

PICASSO

28 LINOGRAPHIES ORIGINALES

DU 4 AVRIL AU 5 MAI 1963

"MADOURA"

LE PLAN - VALLAURIS

IMP. ARNERA - VALLAURIS - Tél. 34.74.55

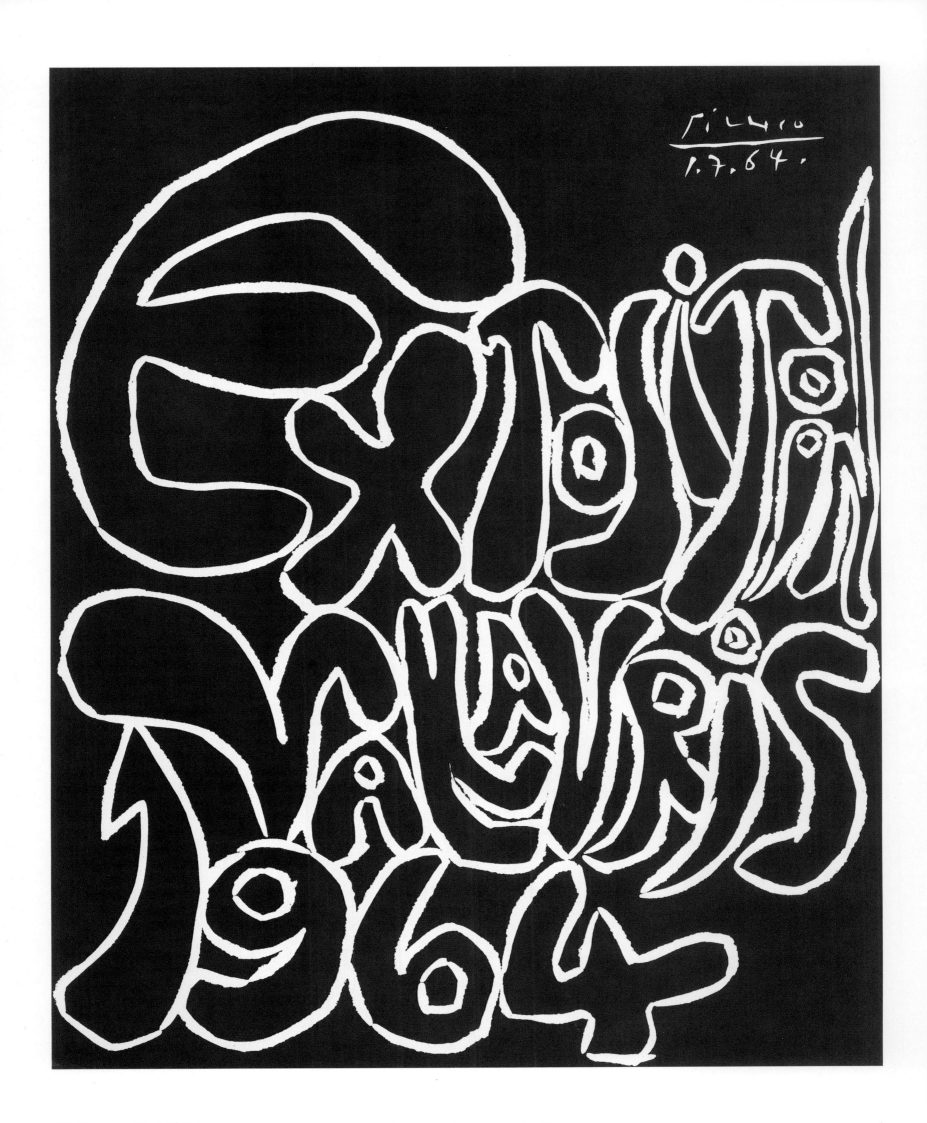

Vallauris Exhibition, 1964
Linocut poster
29⅝×24½ inches (75.2×62.2 cm)
Edition: 168 and 120 impressions on
white Rolo paper and 25 artist's
impressions
The Metropolitan Museum of Art, New

York; The Mr and Mrs Charles Kramer
Collection; Gift of Mr and Mrs Charles
Kramer, 1979

102

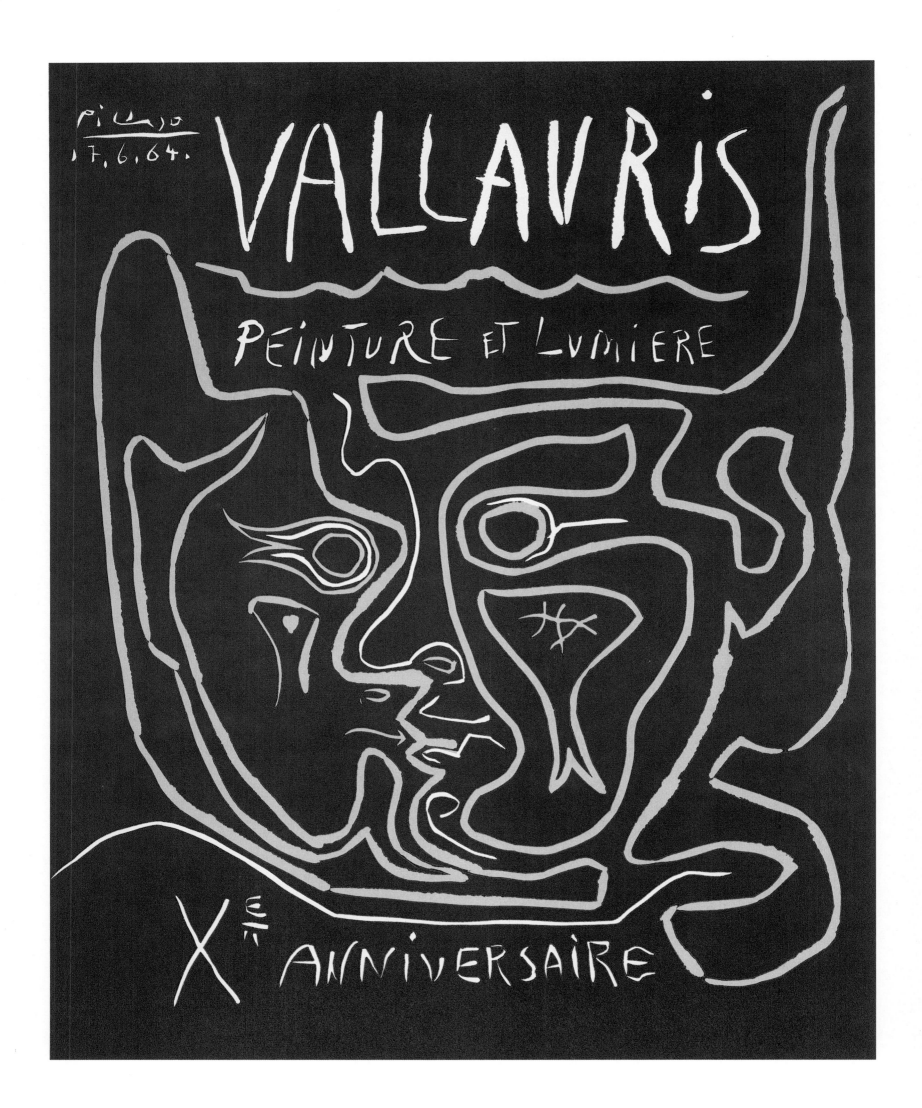

Vallauris Exhibition: 'Painting and Light': Tenth Anniversary, 1964
Linocut poster
29½×24⅜ inches (74.9×61.9 cm)
Edition: 185
The Metropolitan Museum of Art, New York; The Mr and Mrs Charles Kramer Collection; Gift of Mr and Mrs Charles Kramer, 1979

103

Picasso: 85 Prints, 1966
Exhibition poster for Berggruen
Gallery, Paris
Lithograph
29¾×20¾ inches (75.5×51.5 cm)
Edition: 2000
Private Collection

The Blue Owl, 1947
Oil on canvas
48⅜×40¼ inches (123×102 cm)
Private Collection

PICASSO
85 GRAVURES

BERGGRUEN
70 RUE DE L'UNIVERSITÉ - PARIS-VII - 1966

MOURLOT

PICASSO

60 YEARS of GRAPHIC WORKS

28.6.66.

Picasso

Los Angeles County Museum of Art 25 October 24 December 1966

PRINTED IN FRANCE BY MOURLOT - PARIS

Picasso: 60 Years of Graphic Works, 1966
Exhibition poster for the County
Museum, Los Angeles
Lithograph
29⅓×20 inches (74.5×51 cm)
Edition: 2500
Private Collection

Soneto Burlesco, 1947
From Buffon's *Histoire Naturelle*
Etching
14⅛×11 inches (36×28 cm)
Courtesy of the Trustees of the Victoria
and Albert Museum, London

The Bullfight, 1947
Lithograph
11⅝×17 inches (29.5×43 cm)
Courtesy of the Trustees of the Victoria
and Albert Museum, London

Picasso, 1967
Exhibition poster for Galerya
Suvremene Umjetnosti, Zagreb
Serigraph
27¾×20 inches (70.5×51 cm)
Edition: 1020 in Czech and 620 in
German
Private Collection

Picasso

17. 11.-30. 12. 1967.

galerija
suvremene
umjetnosti
zagreb
katarinin trg 2
otvoreno 9.-21 sat

Picasso Posters, 1967
Exhibition poster for Galerie Motte,
Geneva
Photolithograph
30¾×22 inches (78×65 cm)
Edition: 50; additionally 900 prints
without text; 150 prints for the Librairie
Fischbacher, Paris (November 1966);
150 prints for the Grosvenor Gallery,
London (January 1967); 150 prints for
the Gallery of Modern Art, Cologne
(January/February 1967); and 50 prints
for the exhibition at the town of
Offenberg (May/June 1967)
Private Collection

The Woman at the Window,
1952
Aquatint
32¾×18¾ inches (83.3×47.5 cm)
Edition: 50
Courtesy of the Trustees of the Victoria
and Albert Museum, London

GALERIE MOTTE - GENÈVE

10, Quai Général-Guisan

EXPOSITION

PICASSO

(Affiches)

du 16 janvier au 23 février 1968

Acknowledgments

The publisher would like to thank Mike and Sue Rose of Case-bourne Rose who designed this book. We would also like to thank the following agencies, individuals, and institutions for supplying the illustrations:

Art Resource: page 10/Private Collection: page 20
Bettmann Archive: page 14 (above)/Private Collection: page 16 (above)
Christie's London/Bridgeman Art Library: page 90
The Hulton Picture Company: pages 13 (above), 14 (below), 16 (below), 17 (above), 18 (both)
Lords Gallery, London: page 9 (left)/Weidenfeld Archive: page 8
The Metropolitan Museum of Art, New York/Gift of Mr and Mrs Ira Haupt, 1950: page 11/Rogers Fund, 1922: page 13 (below)/The Mr and Mrs Charles Kramer Collection, Gift of Mr and Mrs Charles Kramer, 1979: pages 31, 32, 36, 39, 41, 43, 46, 47, 51, 53, 59, 63, 67, 687, 73, 74, 78, 79, 84, 86-87, 94, 98, 102, 103
Musée des Beaux-Arts, Lyon: page 12

Musée Nationale de la Voiture et du Tourisme, Compiègne/Photo Hutin: page 9 (right)
The Museum of Modern Art, New York/Acquired through the Mrs Sam A Lewisohn Bequest (by exchange) and Mrs Bernard in memory of her husband, Dr Bernard, William Rubin and Anonymous Funds: page 15/Gift of Mrs Simon Guggenheim: page 19
Museo de la Abadia, Monserrat, Catalonia/Bridgeman Art Library: page 70
Mayor Gallery, London/Bridgeman Art Library: page 62
Picasso Museum, Barcelona/Bridgeman Art Library: pages 49, 96/ET Archive: pages 17 (right), 23
Picasso Museum, Paris: 17 (left)
Private Collection: 24, 25, 26, 27, 28, 29, 30, 33, 35, 37, 45, 49, 55, 56, 58, 60, 61, 65, 71, 75, 77, 80, 81, 83, 88, 89, 91, 93, 95, 97, 101, 105, 106, 109, 111, 104/Bridgeman Art Library: page 72
Collection of Mr and Mrs Victor W Ganz, New York: page 22
Courtesy of the Trustees of the Victoria and Albert Museum, London: pages 6, 34, 38, 40, 49, 52, 54, 57, 64, 66, 69, 82, 85, 93, 96, 100, 107, 108, 110